Team Spirit®

THE ATLANTA FALCONS

BY
MARK STEWART

Content Consultant
Jason Aikens

NORWOOD HOUSE PRESS
CHICAGO, ILLINOIS

Norwood House Press
P.O. Box 316598
Chicago, Illinois 60631

For information regarding Norwood House Press, please visit our website at:
www.norwoodhousepress.com or call 866-565-2900.

PHOTO CREDITS:
All photos courtesy Getty Images except the following:
Topps, Inc. (6, 9, 14, 20, 22, 28, 34 left, 37, 38, 40 top & bottom left,
41 right, 43), Black Book Partners (7, 21, 30, 31, 34 right, 35 right),
NASA (29), Author's Collection (36), Matt Richman (48).
Cover photo: Icon SMI
Special thanks to Topps, Inc.

Editor: Mike Kennedy
Designer: Ron Jaffe
Project Management: Black Book Partners, LLC.
Research: Joshua Zaffos
Special thanks to Pete Galbiati

LIBRARY OF CONGRESS CATALOGING-IN-PUBLICATION DATA

Stewart, Mark, 1960-
  The Atlanta Falcons / by Mark Stewart ; content consultant, Jason Aikens.
    p. cm. -- (Team spirit)
  Includes bibliographical references and index.
  Summary: "Presents the history and accomplishments of the Atlanta
Falcons football team. Includes highlights of players, coaches, and awards,
quotes, timeline, maps, glossary and websites"--Provided by publisher.
  ISBN-13: 978-1-59953-328-5 (library edition : alk. paper)
  ISBN-10: 1-59953-328-6 (library edition : alk. paper) 1. Atlanta Falcons
(Football team)--History--Juvenile literature. I. Aikens, Jason. II. Title.

GV956.A85S74 2009
796.332'6409758231--dc22
                                                        2009011900

Manufactured in the United States of America.

COVER PHOTO: The Falcons huddle on offense during a 2009 game.

Table of Contents

SPORTS WORDS & VOCABULARY WORDS: In this book, you will find many words that are new to you. You may also see familiar words used in new ways. The glossary on page 46 gives the meanings of football words, as well as "everyday" words that have special football meanings. These words appear in **bold type** throughout the book. The glossary on page 47 gives the meanings of vocabulary words that are not related to football. They appear in ***bold italic type*** throughout the book.

Meet the Falcons

In the **National Football League (NFL)**, games are usually won and lost at the **line of scrimmage**. Every time the ball is snapped, a contest of strength, speed, and intelligence takes place among huge linemen in a very small space. This is where the Atlanta Falcons have always done their best work. They never stop until the whistle blows.

For the Falcons, when everything is going right in the "trenches," their stars are able to shine. Over the years, the team has had some of the most exciting players in history—powerful runners, *electrifying* receivers, and rifle-armed quarterbacks. Some of the NFL's greatest defensive stars also have worn the Atlanta uniform.

This book tells the story of the Falcons. Few teams have done more to amaze and surprise their fans. The Falcons have had many ups and downs over the years, but the city has always supported them. Perhaps that is why, when football experts expect the least from the Falcons, they have their most thrilling seasons.

Michael Turner breaks free for a big gain during a 2008 game.

Way Back When

Tommy Nobis

During the 1960s, the NFL and **American Football League (AFL)** battled for the hearts of football fans. College football was very popular in the South, and the leagues raced to start a team there. The city of Atlanta, Georgia was in the process of building a modern sports stadium. Fans in the area wanted an NFL team. In 1965, the Falcons were born.

Atlanta built a team using college **draft picks**, unwanted players from other NFL clubs, and **free agents**. But the Falcons struggled in their first season. They lost their first nine games in 1966 and finished at 3–11.

The leader of the Falcons was Tommy Nobis, a linebacker who seemed to be everywhere at once. The big problem for Atlanta was scoring points. The team had some good players on offense—including quarterback Bob Berry and running back Cannonball Butler—but the Falcons were no match for the NFL's top teams.

Slowly but surely, the Falcons improved. Nobis was joined by defensive stars Claude Humphrey, Ken Reaves, and John Zook. Under coach Norm Van Brocklin, the team had a winning record by the early 1970s.

Later in the *decade*, the Falcons found their first offensive star in quarterback Steve Bartkowski. He gave the team confidence whenever he stepped on the field. In 1978, Bartkowski led the Falcons to several last-second victories. Atlanta advanced to the **playoffs** for the first time in team history. In the years that followed, Bartkowski guided a high-scoring offense that featured running back William Andrews and receivers Alfred Jenkins, Wallace Francis, and Junior Miller. In 1980, the Falcons won the **West Division** of the **National Football Conference (NFC)** and reached the playoffs. Two years later, Atlanta advanced to the **postseason** again.

LEFT: Tommy Nobis, the leader of the Falcons in the 1960s.
ABOVE: Steve Bartkowski drops back to pass.

Over the next two decades, the Falcons put more stars on the field, including Gerald Riggs, Jeff George, Chris Miller, Mike Kenn, Bill Fralic, Tony Casillas, Tim McKyer, Andre Rison, Jessie Tuggle, and Bob Whitfield. The most famous of them all was Deion Sanders. He was an amazing defensive back and kick returner with breathtaking speed. Whenever "Prime Time" was near the football, the crowd came alive.

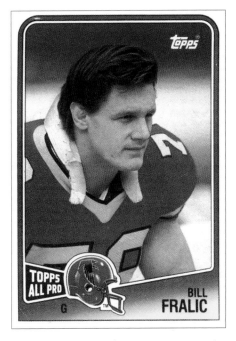

In 1998, the Falcons returned to the top of the NFC West. Coach Dan Reeves guided a **roster** that mixed **veterans** with young stars. The team's leaders included Chris Chandler, Tony Martin, Terance Mathis, Morten Andersen, Eugene Robinson, Jamal Anderson, and Ray Buchanan.

The Falcons called themselves the "Dirty Birds" and had their own special dance. They pecked away at opponents until they won the **NFC Championship** and played in **Super Bowl** XXXIII. For fans in Atlanta, reaching football's biggest game was the ultimate achievement. They couldn't wait to see what the 21st *century* would bring.

LEFT: Deion Sanders, the star defender whose nickname was "Prime Time."   **ABOVE**: A trading card of Bill Fralic, one of the top linemen in team history.

The Team Today

Winning a championship in the NFL requires a combination of talent, timing, and luck. It also takes consistency—playing well game after game, and building on the success of each season. The Falcons have had some of the greatest players ever to wear an NFL uniform. However, they have often struggled to find consistency.

After their trip to Super Bowl XXXIII, the Falcons were weakened by injuries. They sank low in the **standings**. The team rebuilt with exciting young stars such as Michael Vick, Michael Jenkins, Patrick Kerney, Demorrio Williams, and Roddy White. Soon they were back in the playoffs.

In 2007, Atlanta fans were stunned by the news that Vick was out of the picture. He got into trouble away from the field and had to leave the team. The Falcons moved forward. In 2008, they found new young leaders in quarterback Matt Ryan and running back Michael Turner. Atlanta got back to its winning ways and returned to the playoffs. The Falcons were ready for a new *era* of success.

Matt Ryan calls a play at the line of scrimmage during a 2008 game.

Home Turf

The Falcons joined the NFL the same year that baseball's Braves moved to Atlanta from Milwaukee, Wisconsin. The two teams played in Fulton County Stadium starting in 1966. The Falcons stayed there until 1992. That year they moved into a new indoor arena called the Georgia Dome.

For many years, the Georgia Dome was the largest domed structure in the world. It has hosted many different events, including Super Bowls, college basketball games, gymnastics events, and the 1996 Olympics. During a 2008 game, the Georgia Dome was hit by a tornado! Luckily no one was hurt. The Georgia Dome also once hosted a paper airplane competition. The winner set a world record for the longest flight of a paper airplane launched by hand.

BY THE NUMBERS

- *The Falcons' stadium has 71,228 seats for football.*
- *The Atlanta Hawks basketball team once played a game in the dome and drew 62,046 fans.*
- *The Falcons' dome cost $210 million to build.*
- *As of 2009, the Falcons had retired seven numbers—10 (Steve Bartkowski), 31 (William Andrews), 57 (Jeff Van Note), 58 (Jessie Tuggle), 60 (Tommy Nobis), 78 (Mike Kenn), and 87 (Claude Humphrey).*

Fans fill the Georgia Dome for a Falcons game in 2007.

Dressed for Success

Ollege football is a big deal in Georgia. Two of the state's most popular schools are the University of Georgia and Georgia Tech. When the Falcons chose their uniform design, they borrowed colors from these two colleges. The Falcons used Georgia's deep red and Georgia Tech's white, black, and gold.

The look of Atlanta's uniform has changed over the years, but the basic colors have remained the same. Only the gold is gone. Also, in 1990, the team changed from red helmets to black ones.

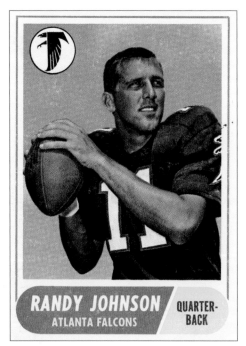

Atlanta's **logo** shows a falcon in flight. It has been used on the team's helmet since 1966. When the logo was unveiled in the 1960s, people said it looked **futuristic**. They were right—more than 40 years later, it has hardly changed at all. Today's logo is a little more modern than the old one.

Randy Johnson models the team's uniform from the late 1960s. The Atlanta logo is in the top left corner.

RANDY JOHNSON
ATLANTA FALCONS
QUARTER-
BACK

UNIFORM BASICS

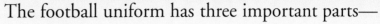

The football uniform has three important parts—
- Helmet
- Jersey
- Pants

Helmets used to be made out of leather, and they did not have facemasks—ouch! Today, helmets are made of super-strong plastic. The uniform top, or jersey, is made of thick fabric. It fits snugly around a player so that tacklers cannot grab it and pull him down. The pants come down just over the knees.

There is a lot more to a football uniform than what you see on the outside. Air can be pumped inside the helmet to give it a snug, padded fit. The jersey covers shoulder pads, and sometimes a rib protector called a flak jacket. The pants include pads that protect the hips, thighs, *tailbone*, and knees.

Football teams have two sets of uniforms—one dark and one light. This makes it easier to tell two teams apart on the field. Almost all teams wear their dark uniforms at home and their light ones on the road.

Jerious Norwood heads downfield in Atlanta's 2008 home uniform.

We Won!

T he Falcons promised their fans a new era of success when they hired Dan Reeves to coach the team in 1997. Eight games into the season, it looked like nothing had changed. Atlanta's record stood at 1–7. But just when everyone was about to give up on the club, something amazing happened. The players began believing in themselves and their coach. And they began to win.

Quarterback Chris Chandler, who was hurt much of the year, got healthy and started throwing touchdown passes. Running back Jamal Anderson gained confidence and ended up rushing for more than 1,000 yards. The Atlanta defense started punishing opponents with hard hits and **quarterback sacks**. The Falcons won six of their final eight games. Heading into 1998, they felt as if they could beat anyone.

They were right. That season the Falcons lost only twice. Chandler threw 25 touchdown passes. Anderson led the NFC with 1,846 rushing yards and 14 touchdowns, and set an NFL record with 410 carries. The defense—led by Chuck Smith, Lester Archambeau, Shane Dronett, Cornelius Bennett, Jessie Tuggle, Ray Buchanan, and Eugene Robinson—made opponents work hard for their points. When Reeves announced to his players that he needed to have open-heart surgery, they kept on winning until he returned to full health.

Reeves was back on the sidelines for the Falcons' first playoff game, at home against the San Francisco 49ers. San Francisco had been the top dog in the NFC West for a long time. Now the "Dirty Birds" would have their revenge.

LEFT: Chris Chandler fires a pass during the 1998 season.
ABOVE: Chuck Smith celebrates a great defensive play.

Anderson scored twice in the first half. Atlanta's defense kept quarterback Steve Young from mounting a *comeback*. The Falcons won 20–18 to reach the NFC Championship for the first time in their history.

Atlanta's defense would be put to the test against the Minnesota Vikings. They had a record-smashing offense that starred Randy Moss, Cris Carter, Robert Smith, and Randall Cunningham. The Falcons scored first, but the Vikings answered with two touchdowns and two **field goals** to take a 20–7 lead. The Falcons weren't done. They forced a **fumble** by Minnesota and scored right before halftime to keep the game close at 20–14.

The Vikings led 27–17 in the fourth quarter. Anderson was not finding much room to run, and Chandler was limping because of an injury. But the Falcons came alive in the final minutes. The Vikings had a chance to put the contest out of reach, but they missed a field goal. When Atlanta got the ball back, Chandler drove the Falcons 71 yards for the game-tying touchdown.

The two teams went into **overtime**. Neither could score at first. The second time the Falcons had the ball, they moved close enough for Morten Andersen to try a 38-yard field goal. His kick was good, and the Falcons were NFC champs. Nothing could keep the fans in Atlanta from enjoying this historic victory—not even a loss to the Denver Broncos in Super Bowl XXXIII.

LEFT: Shane Dronett and Cornelius Bennett team up to tackle Steve Young during the 1998 playoffs.   **ABOVE**: Jamal Anderson leads coach Dan Reeves and the rest of the team in the "Dirty Bird" dance after their win over the Minnesota Vikings.

Go-To Guys

To be a true star in the NFL, you need more than fast feet and a big body. You have to be a "go-to guy"—someone the coach wants on the field at the end of a big game. Fans of the Falcons have had a lot to cheer about over the years, including these great stars …

THE PIONEERS

TOMMY NOBIS   Linebacker

• BORN: 9/20/1943   • PLAYED FOR TEAM: 1966 TO 1976

Hard-hitting Tommy Nobis was the first pure linebacker ever taken with the first pick in the NFL draft. He did not disappoint Atlanta fans. In his first season, he made 294 tackles! Nobis was selected to play in the **Pro Bowl** five times during his NFL career.

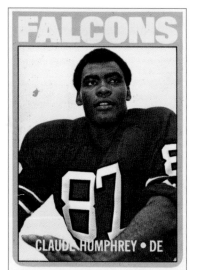

CLAUDE HUMPHREY   Defensive Lineman

• BORN: 6/29/1944   • PLAYED FOR TEAM: 1968 TO 1978

Claude Humphrey was a fierce pass rusher. He was voted to the **All-Pro** team eight times. In 1977, Humphrey starred on the Atlanta defense that set a modern record by giving up just 9.2 points per game.

ABOVE: Claude Humphrey   **RIGHT**: Mike Kenn

JEFF VAN NOTE   Offensive Lineman

• BORN: 2/7/1946   • PLAYED FOR TEAM: 1969 TO 1986

Jeff Van Note played running back in college, but the Falcons decided he would make a better center. They were right. He played 18 years for Atlanta and was voted the team's all-time favorite player by the fans.

STEVE BARTKOWSKI   Quarterback

• BORN: 11/12/1952   • PLAYED FOR TEAM: 1975 TO 1985

The Falcons used the first pick in the 1975 draft on Steve Bartkowski. He used his powerful arm to win **Rookie of the Year**. In 1980 and 1981, Bartkowski became one of very few NFL quarterbacks to throw at least 30 touchdown passes two seasons in a row.

MIKE KENN   Offensive Lineman

• BORN: 2/9/1956   • PLAYED FOR TEAM: 1978 TO 1994

Mike Kenn was a mountain-sized lineman. He stood 6′ 7″ and weighed 286 pounds. Kenn was the NFL's finest tackle during the early 1980s. He set a team record for games played with 251. Later he became a successful politician.

WILLIAM ANDREWS   Running Back

• BORN: 12/25/1955   • PLAYED FOR TEAM: 1979 TO 1983 & 1986

William Andrews did everything for the Falcons. He rushed for more than 1,000 yards four times, caught 277 passes in six years, and was one of the best blockers in the NFL. Teammates and fans respected him for his consistency and the way he battled injuries.

JESSIE TUGGLE   Linebacker

- BORN: 4/4/1965
- PLAYED FOR TEAM: 1987 TO 2000

Teammates called Jessie Tuggle the "Hammer" for his hard hits. He made more than 1,800 tackles in an Atlanta uniform. Tuggle was also known for scooping up fumbles. He returned three for touchdowns during his career.

DEION SANDERS   Defensive Back/ Kick & Punt Returner

- BORN: 8/9/1967
- PLAYED FOR TEAM: 1989 TO 1993

When Deion Sanders covered a receiver, quarterbacks rarely even attempted to throw a pass his way. Sanders led the NFC in **interceptions** twice. He also returned two punts and three kickoffs for touchdowns for the Falcons.

PATRICK KERNEY   Defensive Lineman

- BORN: 12/30/1976   • PLAYED FOR TEAM: 1999 TO 2006

Opponents were never sure where Patrick Kerney would line up or what he would do. That made him a scary player, especially for quarterbacks. Kerney's teammates were also *wary* of him. When he wasn't sacking quarterbacks, he was famous for his practical jokes and weird costumes.

MICHAEL VICK   Quarterback

- BORN: 6/26/1980 • PLAYED FOR TEAM: 2001 TO 2006

Michael Vick might have been the fastest man ever to play quarterback. He used his speed and strong arm to become one of the NFL's most exciting players. Vick set an NFL record in 2006 with a rushing average of 8.45 yards per carry.

ALGE CRUMPLER   Tight End

- BORN: 12/23/1977 • PLAYED FOR TEAM: 2001 TO 2007

Alge Crumpler's father and brother played in the NFL, but he was by far the most famous of the three. A good blocker and pass-catcher, Crumpler was selected to play in the Pro Bowl each year from 2003 to 2006.

MATT RYAN   Quarterback

- BORN: 5/17/1985

- FIRST SEASON WITH TEAM: 2008

Rookie quarterbacks often struggle in the NFL—not Matt Ryan. His first pass was a 62-yard touchdown to Michael Jenkins. He finished his rookie season with 3,440 passing yards and 16 touchdowns. Ryan led the Falcons to the playoffs that year and set a rookie record with 26 completions in his first postseason game.

LEFT: Jessie Tuggle
RIGHT: Matt Ryan

On the Sidelines

The Falcons have one of the strangest records in sports. From 1966 to 2008—a span of 43 seasons—the team never had a winning record two years in a row. Needless to say, they went through a lot of coaches during that time!

Atlanta's best "sideline *strategists*" included Norm Van Brocklin, Marion Campbell, Jerry Glanville, June Jones, Dan Reeves, Jim Mora, and Mike Smith. Glanville was famous for driving race cars and leaving tickets at the box office for Elvis Presley, who had died many years earlier. It was fun to be a Falcon when he was in charge.

Reeves was more serious about his job. He underwent heart surgery during the 1998 season and returned to coach the team three weeks later! That year he guided the Falcons to the Super Bowl.

The team's best coach may have been Leeman Bennett. He was an expert in the passing game when he came to Atlanta in 1977. That season, however, the Falcons became famous for their defense. They called themselves the "Grits Blitz" and set a record by allowing just 129 points in 14 games. In 1980, Bennett led the Falcons to their first NFC West title.

Leeman Bennett, the coach who led the Falcons to the first division title in team history.

One Great Day

Atlanta fans did not have much to cheer about during the Falcons' early years. One losing season followed another. The 1978 season looked like another disappointment. The team lost four of its first six games. But then the Falcons caught fire and went on a winning streak. Their fans began dreaming of making the playoffs.

That dream turned into a nightmare during a November game against the New Orleans Saints. The Falcons trailed 17–6 with less than three minutes left. Their season was on the line. Steve Bartkowski led the team on an 80-yard touchdown drive to make the score 17–13. The Falcons then tried an **onside kick**, hoping to get the ball back. The play failed, and the Saints took possession.

Time was working against the Falcons. All the Saints had to do was make a first down and watch the time on the clock run out. The Atlanta defense was ready. The Falcons stopped New Orleans on four running plays and regained possession of the ball with just a few seconds left. They were 57 yards from the goal line.

Bartkowski called a play known as "Big Ben Right." Three receivers lined up on the right side and sprinted toward the end zone.

Steve Bartkowski prepares to launch a long pass.

Bartkowski heaved the ball high in the air. Atlanta's Wallace Francis and Alfred Jenkins positioned themselves at the goal line to catch the pass.

Francis jumped and tipped the ball. Jenkins saw the ball tumbling through the air and snagged it before it hit the turf. The Falcons scored the winning touchdown! Atlanta went on to reach the playoffs.

To this day, Big Ben Right is the most famous play in team history. "There was no primary receiver," Francis said afterward. "We just batted the ball around and hoped someone would catch it. Seriously, that's what we do."

"I just throw it up and hope!" Bartkowski admitted.

Legend Has It

Which Falcon gained 1,000 yards in a season—only to finish with less than that?

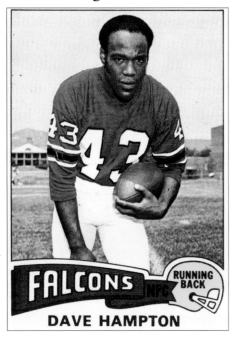

FALCONS **NFC** RUNNING BACK

DAVE HAMPTON

LEGEND HAS IT that Dave Hampton did. In a game against the Kansas City Chiefs on the final day of the 1972 season, Hampton became the first player in Atlanta history to rush for 1,000 yards. The contest was halted, and he was presented with the ball as a *symbol* of his achievement. When the game *resumed*, coach Norm Van Brocklin sent Hampton back into play. On his first carry, he lost six yards. Hampton got the ball once more but gained only one yard. He finished the season with 995 yards. In 1975, Hampton topped 1,000 yards again. This time the Falcons were smart—they pulled him out of the game!

ABOVE: Dave Hampton
RIGHT: Astronaut Frank Borman gets ready for a mission.

Which Falcons star got career advice from outer space?

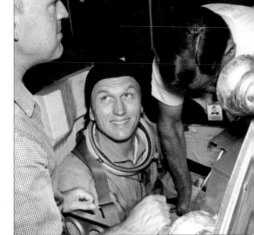

LEGEND HAS IT that Tommy Nobis did. However, he ignored it! In November of 1965, Nobis was drafted by the Falcons and the Houston Oilers of the AFL. While he was deciding between the teams, two orbiting NASA astronauts sent him a message. Frank Borman radioed to Mission Control in Houston: "Tell Nobis to sign with the Oilers!" Nobis wasn't convinced. He later signed with the Falcons.

Which Falcon once threw a football entirely out of a stadium?

LEGEND HAS IT that Michael Vick did. But in this case, the legend is wrong! Vick's famous throw—which was part of a Powerade commercial—was helped by computer animation. Several decades earlier, however, Steve Bartkowski actually did throw a ball out of Memorial Stadium in Baltimore. The rocket-armed quarterback stood on the goal line and fired two passes toward the top of the stands. The first one fell short. The second soared out of the stadium and landed in the street outside.

It Really Happened

Most **professional** football players are **versatile** athletes. However, by the time they reach the NFL, they have decided to give up on all other sports. When Deion Sanders joined the Falcons in 1989, he had not yet made that choice. In fact, Sanders was already playing baseball for the New York Yankees that season. He missed training camp and had time for just two practices before his first NFL game.

The player known as "Prime Time" showed that he was a rare talent. After just a few minutes in a Falcons uniform, he caught a

LEFT: Deion Sanders takes a break during a Falcons game.　**RIGHT**: "Prime Time" wears his Braves uniform.

punt and ran 68 yards through the Los Angeles Rams for a touchdown. A few days earlier, Sanders had slugged a home run for the Yankees. He was the first person to hit a home run and score an NFL touchdown in the same week.

The legend of "Prime Time" grew and grew. He became one of the best players in history. His tremendous speed and great moves gave him a chance to score every time he touched the ball. Meanwhile, he became a star in baseball too. After a trade to the Atlanta Braves—who played just a couple of miles away from the Falcons—Sanders batted .300 and led his league in triples.

On October 10th, 1992, Sanders was on the field for a playoff game with the Braves in Pittsburgh. The next afternoon he was on the field for the Falcons in a game against the Miami Dolphins. After the football game, Sanders jumped back on a plane for Pittsburgh and suited up for the Braves again that evening!

Team Spirit

Few cities have ever supported a football team the way Atlanta has. The Falcons put their first tickets on sale on November 1st, 1965. In less than two months, the team had sold 45,000 **season tickets**. To this day, Atlanta fans make Falcons home games very difficult for opponents because of all the noise they create.

The Falcons have had many faithful fans over the years. One of the most famous was Joe Curtis. He almost never missed a game. Curtis was in the stands for every home game (and many road games) for more than 35 years—or more than 400 games in all!

For most of those years, Freddie Falcon has been entertaining the fans. He is one of the most popular *mascots* in the NFL. Freddie not only appears at Falcons games, he has shown up at the Pro Bowl and Super Bowl. He has also traveled overseas to meet members of the military. Freddie is joined at home games by the Atlanta Falcons Cheerleaders. They perform for fans in red-white-and-black uniforms that match the colors the players wear.

Harry Douglas celebrates with fans after a touchdown during a 2008 game.

Timeline

In this timeline, each Super Bowl is listed under the year it was played. Remember that the Super Bowl is held early in the year and is actually part of the previous season. For example, Super Bowl XLIII was played on February 1st, 2009, but it was the championship of the 2008 NFL season.

1971
Claude Humphrey is named All-Pro.

1980
The Falcons are NFC West champs for the first time.

1966
The Falcons join the NFL as an **expansion team**.

1978
The Falcons make the playoffs for the first time.

1985
Gerald Riggs leads the NFC in rushing.

Alfred Jenkins, a star for the 1978 and 1980 teams.

Gerald Riggs

Matt
Ryan

1998
Jamal Anderson sets an NFL
record with 410 carries—and
invents the "Dirty Bird" dance!

2008
Matt Ryan is named
Rookie of the Year.

1995
Eric Metcalf sets a
team record with
104 receptions.

1999
Tim Dwight scores Atlanta's
first Super Bowl touchdown
on a 94-yard kickoff return.

2006
Michael Vick is the first
quarterback to rush for
1,000 yards.

Eric
Metcalf

Michael
Vick

Fun Facts

SURE-HANDED

In 1985, Gerald Riggs carried the ball 379 times and caught 33 passes. He did not fumble once all year.

FLY PATTERN

For Atlanta's first home game in 1966, the team trained a live falcon to circle the stadium three times and then return to its trainer. On game day, it flew around the stadium once and then flew away, never to be seen again.

LITTLE-KNOWN STORY

In 1980 and 1981, Reggie Smith returned punts and kickoffs for the Falcons. At 5′ 4″, he was the shortest player in the NFL.

WELCOME TO THE TEAM

In 2008, the Falcons signed running back Michael Turner as a free agent. He ran for 220 yards on opening day. Turner set a record for most yards gained by a player in his first game for a new team.

MAXIMUM WAGES

In a 1969 game against the New Orleans Saints, running back Harmon Wages did it all for the Falcons. He threw for a touchdown in the first quarter, caught a touchdown pass in the second quarter, and ran for a touchdown in the third quarter.

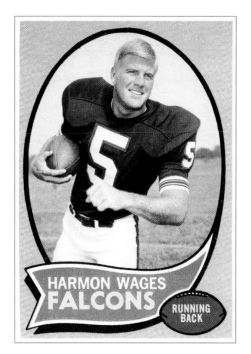

HAMMER TIME

In 1991, Deion Sanders, Andre Rison, and coach Jerry Glanville appeared in the MC Hammer video "Too Legit to Quit." The song rose to the sixth most popular in the country.

BATTLING BROTHERS

In 1975 and 1976, the four games between the Falcons and San Francisco 49ers featured a kicking battle between two brothers. Atlanta's Nick Mike-Mayer lost the battle of field goals to Steve Mike-Mayer of the 49ers, but the Falcons won three of the four games.

LEFT: A button from the team's first season.
ABOVE: Harmon Wages

Talking Football

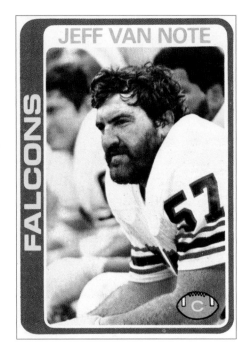

JEFF VAN NOTE

FALCONS

57

"I'm proud of the fact that I'm an Atlanta Falcon."

—Matt Ryan, on becoming the team's quarterback in 2008

"I remember **distinctly** thinking as a rookie that I might not even last a year."

—Jeff Van Note, who ended up playing 18 years for the Falcons

"I've always wanted to be the best."

—Andre Rison, on what drove him to become a star

"It used to upset me that I never got to play in a postseason game. Suddenly, now, the cloud is lifted."

—Tommy Nobis, after watching the Falcons win the 1998 NFC Championship

ABOVE: Jeff Van Note
RIGHT: Jerry Glanville

"I don't care how many snaps you play, everyone leaves a little of himself on that field. It goes with the territory of being an ex-NFL quarterback."

—*Steve Bartkowski, on the stress of playing pro football*

"I always built the defense around outside linebackers that could pressure the passer."

—*Jerry Glanville, on his plan as head coach of the Falcons*

"The key to being a good head coach is getting a good feel on the pulse of your football team."

—*Dan Reeves, on the importance of communicating with the players*

"I knew the Atlanta Falcons would someday get to the Super Bowl. But I didn't know if I'd still be here."

—*Jessie Tuggle, who played in Super Bowl XXXIII in his 12th season with the team*

For the Record

T he great Falcons teams and players have left their marks on the record books. These are the "best of the best" ...

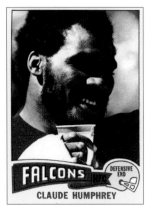

Claude Humphrey

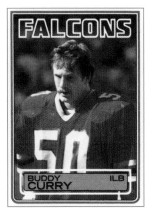

Buddy Curry

FALCONS AWARD WINNERS

WINNER	AWARD	YEAR
Claude Humphrey	Defensive Rookie of the Year	1968
Buddy Curry	co-Defensive Rookie of the Year	1980
Al Richardson	co-Defensive Rookie of the Year	1980
Andre Rison	Pro Bowl Most Valuable Player*	1994
Dan Reeves	Coach of the Year	1998
Matt Ryan	Offensive Rookie of the Year	2008
Mike Smith	Coach of the Year	2008

* The Most Valuable Player award is given to each season's best player and the best player in the Super Bowl and Pro Bowl.

Andre Rison

FALCONS ACHIEVEMENTS

ACHIEVEMENT	YEAR
NFC West Champions	1980
NFC West Champions	1998
NFC Champions	1998
NFC South Champions	2004

NFC PRO BOWL
WILLIAM ANDREWS RB

ABOVE: A trading card of William Andrews, one of the stars of the 1980 NFC West champs.

LEFT: Kicker Morten Andersen watches as his overtime field goal wins the 1998 NFC Championship for the Falcons.

Pinpoints

T he history of a football team is made up of many smaller stories. These stories take place all over the map—not just in the city a team calls "home." Match the pushpins on these maps to the Team Facts and you will begin to see the story of the Falcons unfold!

TEAM FACTS

1   Atlanta, Georgia—*The Falcons have played here since 1966.*

2   Quincy, Florida—*Cannonball Butler was born here.*

3   Memphis, Tennessee—*Claude Humphrey was born here.*

4   Exton, Pennsylvania—*Matt Ryan was born here.*

5   Trenton, New Jersey—*Patrick Kerney was born here.*

6   Flint, Michigan—*Andre Rison was born here.*

7   Des Moines, Iowa—*Steve Bartkowski was born here.*

8   Tullos, Louisiana—*Gerald Riggs was born here.*

9   San Antonio, Texas—*Tommy Nobis was born here.*

10   Garden City, Kansas—*John Zook was born here.*

11   San Jose, California—*Bob Berry was born here.*

12   Bologna, Italy—*Nick Mike-Mayer was born here.*

John Zook

Play Ball

Football is a sport played by two teams on a field that is 100 yards long. The game is divided into four 15-minute quarters. Each team must have 11 players on the field at all times. The group that has the ball is called the offense. The group trying to keep the offense from moving the ball forward is called the defense.

A football game is made up of a series of "plays." Each play starts and ends with a referee's signal. A play begins when the center snaps the ball between his legs to the quarterback. The quarterback then gives the ball to a teammate, throws (or "passes") the ball to a teammate, or runs with the ball himself. The job of the defense is to tackle the player with the ball or stop the quarterback's pass. A play ends when the ball (or player holding the ball) is "down." The offense must move the ball forward at least 10 yards every four downs. If it fails to do so, the other team is given the ball. If the offense has not made 10 yards after three downs—and does not want to risk losing the ball—it can kick (or "punt") the ball to make the other team start from its own end of the field.

At each end of a football field is a goal line, which divides the field from the end zone. A team must run or pass the ball over the goal line to score a touchdown, which counts for six points. After scoring a touchdown, a team can try a short kick for one "extra point," or try again to run or pass across the goal line for two points. Teams can score three points from anywhere on the field by kicking the ball between the goal posts. This is called a field goal.

The defense can score two points if it tackles a player while he is in his own end zone. This is called a safety. The defense can also score points by taking the ball away from the offense and crossing the opposite goal line for a touchdown. The team with the most points after 60 minutes is the winner.

Football may seem like a very hard game to understand, but the more you play and watch football, the more "little things" you are likely to notice. The next time you are at a game, look for these plays:

PLAY LIST

BLITZ—A play in which the defense sends extra tacklers after the quarterback. If the quarterback sees a blitz coming, he passes the ball quickly. If he does not, he can end up at the bottom of a very big pile!

DRAW—A play in which the offense pretends it will pass the ball, and then gives it to a running back. If the offense can "draw" the defense to the quarterback and his receivers, the running back should have lots of room to run.

FLY PATTERN—A play in which a team's fastest receiver is told to "fly" past the defensive backs for a long pass. Many long touchdowns are scored on this play.

SQUIB KICK—A play in which the ball is kicked a short distance on purpose. A squib kick is used when the team kicking off does not want the other team's fastest player to catch the ball and run with it.

SWEEP—A play in which the ball carrier follows a group of teammates moving sideways to "sweep" the defense out of the way. A good sweep gives the runner a chance to gain a lot of yards before he is tackled or forced out of bounds.

Glossary

FOOTBALL WORDS TO KNOW

ALL-PRO—An honor given to the best players at their position at the end of each season.

AMERICAN FOOTBALL LEAGUE (AFL)—The football league that began play in 1960 and later merged with the NFL.

DRAFT PICKS—College players selected or "drafted" by NFL teams each spring.

EXPANSION TEAM—A team added to a league when it expands.

FIELD GOALS—Goals from the field, kicked over the crossbar and between the goal posts. A field goal is worth three points.

FREE AGENTS—Players who are allowed to sign with any team that wants them.

FUMBLE—A ball that is dropped by the player carrying it.

INTERCEPTIONS—Passes that are caught by the defensive team.

LINE OF SCRIMMAGE—The imaginary line that separates the offense and defense before each play begins.

NATIONAL FOOTBALL CONFERENCE (NFC)—One of two groups of teams that make up the NFL. The winner of the NFC plays the winner of the American Football Conference (AFC) in the Super Bowl.

NATIONAL FOOTBALL LEAGUE (NFL)—The league that started in 1920 and is still operating today.

NFC CHAMPIONSHIP—The game played to determine which NFC team will go to the Super Bowl.

ONSIDE KICK—A short kickoff that the kicking team tries to recover.

OVERTIME—The extra period played when a game is tied after 60 minutes.

PLAYOFFS—The games played after the season to determine which teams play in the Super Bowl.

POSTSEASON—Another term for playoffs.

PRO BOWL—The NFL's all-star game, played after the Super Bowl.

PROFESSIONAL—A player or team that plays a sport for money.

QUARTERBACK SACKS—Tackles of the quarterback behind the line of scrimmage.

ROOKIE OF THE YEAR—The annual award given to the league's best first-year player.

ROSTER—The list of a team's active players.

SEASON TICKETS—Packages of tickets for each home game.

STANDINGS—A list of teams, starting with the team with the best record and ending with the team with the worst record.

SUPER BOWL—The championship of football, played between the winners of the NFC and AFC.

VETERANS—Players with great experience.

WEST DIVISION—A division for teams that play in the western part of the country.

OTHER WORDS TO KNOW

CENTURY—A period of 100 years.

COMEBACK—The process of catching up from behind, or making up a large deficit.

DECADE—A period of 10 years; also specific periods, such as the 1950s.

DISTINCTLY—Clearly and plainly.

ELECTRIFYING—Very exciting.

ERA—A period of time in history.

FUTURISTIC—Having or involving modern technology or design.

LOGO—A symbol or design that represents a company or team.

MASCOTS—Animals or people believed to bring a group good luck.

RESUMED—Began again after a break.

STRATEGISTS—People who develop plans or methods for succeeding.

SYMBOL—Something that represents a thought or idea.

TAILBONE—The bone that protects the base of the spine.

VERSATILE—Able to do many things well.

WARY—Cautious or careful.

Places to Go

ON THE ROAD

ATLANTA FALCONS
1 Georgia Dome Drive, NW
Atlanta, Georgia 30313
(770) 965-3115

THE PRO FOOTBALL HALL OF FAME
2121 George Halas Drive NW
Canton, Ohio 44708
(330) 456-8207

ON THE WEB

THE NATIONAL FOOTBALL LEAGUE   www.nfl.com
  • *Learn more about the National Football League*

THE ATLANTA FALCONS   www.atlantafalcons.com
  • *Learn more about the Atlanta Falcons*

THE PRO FOOTBALL HALL OF FAME   www.profootballhof.com
  • *Learn more about football's greatest players*

ON THE BOOKSHELF

To learn more about the sport of football, look for these books at your library or bookstore:

  • Stewart, Mark and Kennedy, Mike. *Touchdown: the Power and Precision of Football's Perfect Play*. Minneapolis, Minnesota: Millbrook Press, 2009.

  • Buckley Jr., James. *The Child's World Encyclopedia of the NFL*. Mankato, Minnesota: Child's World, 2008.

  • Gigliotti, Jim. *Football*. Ann Arbor, Michigan: Cherry Lake Publishing, 2009.

  • Jacobs, Greg. *The Everything Kids' Football Book: the all-time greats, legendary teams, today's superstars—and tips on playing like a pro*. Cincinnati, Ohio: Adams Media, 2008.

Index

PAGE NUMBERS IN **BOLD** REFER TO ILLUSTRATIONS.

The Team

MARK STEWART has written more than 50 books on football, and over 200 sports books for kids. He grew up in New York City during the 1960s rooting for the Giants and Jets, and now takes his two daughters, Mariah and Rachel, to watch them play in their home state of New Jersey. Mark comes from a family of  writers. His grandfather was Sunday Editor of *The New York Times* and his mother was Articles Editor of *The Ladies' Home Journal* and *McCall's*. Mark has profiled hundreds of athletes over the last 20 years. He has also written several books about New York and New Jersey. Mark is a graduate of Duke University, with a degree in History. He lives with his daughters and wife Sarah overlooking Sandy Hook, New Jersey.

JASON AIKENS is the Collections Curator at the Pro Football Hall of Fame. He is responsible for the preservation of the Pro Football Hall of Fame's collection of artifacts and memorabilia and obtaining new donations of memorabilia from current players and NFL teams. Jason has a Bachelor of Arts in History from Michigan State University and a Master's in History from Western Michigan University where he concentrated on sports history. Jason  has been working for the Pro Football Hall of Fame since 1997; before that he was an intern at the College Football Hall of Fame. Jason's family has roots in California and has been following the St. Louis Rams since their days in Los Angeles, California. He lives with his wife Cynthia and their daughter Angelina in Canton, Ohio.